SKY JOURNAL

SKY JOURNAL

Hassen Saker

Gina —
Happy to now know
you. Hope you find
something of value in this
book-thing!
xo hassen

27 Sept 14 DUSIE

Poems have appeared in the following publications: *Dusie, TOOL, Newport Life Magazine* and *BIG BRIDGE.*

Many thanks to those who inspired or made this 10-year project possible: Lynne Omenson, Susan Minyard, Jenna Leahy, Joel Lirot, and Jared Hassen. Also deep thanks to Ethel Rackin, Colleen Hammond, and Thomas Devaney.

Cover art: *Postage Due*, Colleen Hammond

Layout and Book Design by DUSIE
dusie.org | Kingston, RI

First printing, Hassen Saker 2014

ISBN-13: 978-0-9819808-8-1

I found myself, in other words, constructing a geometry, a geometry of things that had no geometry. *Benoit Mandelbrot*

CONTENTS

FROM LAND

elevation

close your eyes
    open them

    planes count ten years or ten minutes

glory

from the west a bird expands
one line of breath extending

let that sense

forgive me for choices
my eyes roll
hadn't everything gone right

children don't return
dark fields of night instead

how to measure
electricity of transformation

cold rain for days
sky broke on sunday
all around the world
we engage monsters
but not as much as monsters
we speak   how our rapport
constructs from many decompositions
blue ring venom for instance

encourage galileo to stay away from here
until things blow over

nostalgic for assurance
question the foundation of every art

to be nameless or allowed it
sensation of specific chemical formulae (truth)
circling empty blocks   traffic lights
cycle my yellow steps red green

am i too everything

repeating words
under black-blue evening bags
to believe them

nothing blemished
smear over head
funnel touches
surface easily deflects
each superficial devastation
only a handful of inscriptions

oh this sight
grays blues anvil head sweeping and the original
name

silent walk
nothing to present
so little dark
precipitation circumscribes light

wind battered panes

the end of play   go in
without the buzz heavier
without

tell me the fowl secret of you
corona

is it that you can't think
clear of futility of cycles like your music

my mouth

get down do something

thunderheads a hundred miles away
here smooth white planes of cloud stay with us
hundreds of miles of solid sky

if i saw you you wouldn't be there
under that oak tree

in the field of grass miles below

seven   *dad how far can we see*
wanted to look after
my heart where it sped ahead

left marginal interest
staid in the box
most fear dust of nothing determinate
i do realize the crusade of walls
it's very cirrus

your cold eye permission to express
in your black on white   disposable skin
rep like that   unfortunate
care   caught a bullet
compact sternum   carry on
reach beneath the sheet to care less
twisted leg and water does no good
beating against stone featherless

plane of situation

i like now

when flooding
map the green indication
(severity) interpretation
(serenity)
close friends subtly dry out (love cry)
rich man find the way
my indirect navigation takes more than a lifetime
phosphorous biolife whisper mum's the word
and my succulent thought bastes in it
so go ask the amount of rainfall nothing can
intimidate me now

full orb clouds curtain
chorus of earthworms
leaves crackle into soul jaw mute finger
moths mention prison wearing you down
not enough cerulean mathematics

now how to dredge the distressed
heavens of my jettisoned words

target

complete zero

womb

pod

planet

eye

fruit

brain

ball

bubble

complete period

petulant heavens
        over cast
breaks phantasmagoric (rather not)
brilliant strikes into actual flesh and burning
how the virtual can destroy the real

my bare arm rolls you over
or protects your head
nothing like a storm to accent the breast

celestial brush
root of desire
shades of azure
to which i aspire
take this racket or none
screeching screech

theory yet under noctilucent

warn high flying fowl of sunrise
how high geese over common clouds
ducks or crystallized spiders

floating indefinitely i've heard
again the question convolutes or mutates from
essential
        will it end or be worthwhile
          what's the limit

        stay away from the study of thought, son

he'd said the universe fit us

how are we so *solute*
with bees and wasps
twigs and cars

how could his mind
come from a seed
ready to roll

aspiring to a directed silence
    what they say
    while eye & floating cataracts
    my patience
    nothing novel
    guess my hand held
    inside sidewalk wide eyed
    how does the moon
    enter an isolated world
    or finally light a solitary path
    or how the small heart explodes
    beneath a brilliant eye
    projector   predator   *bone of bone*

           hued cirrus
           graduate back
           from the sunset

spectral timer
the stretch of lit tendrils

how i'm some thing more and less skin
mostly of the back
told the age of lovers and their earnest attention

    ethereal invertebrates
    we beautifully form and beautifully dissipate

slow going
mess through fall in leaf bed to oh, where I left off
love blinks fifteen years
mysterious ink
calligraphy reappears
if something bad happens
as the long ago lover flying at first chance to spend
one night
oh the urgency of fire at fathoms
what to me now   that measure
autumn wind dies down limbs crashing

altar state

fine tune

vedic

rain again recent
a rock I've loved   all heart
anemone
harriet tubman
farsi

even an ideologue
ideal cloud ideal god
uncapped clouds

body aqua *effervescent* at that thought

j u m p i n g   b e a n s
sanguineous

working the ruins weather taps the window pane
days are so small they avert approaching habits
locations meld netherworld homes
search for cures travelers buzz chaos recipe
rumpled clothes history's emergency
siren aggravation chasing ghosts off
object jets out the window
throat's angle

evidence is all talk
motive course absent
stars, breathing holes
stars, branding irons

blue threat spread on the line
what i've never seen before
ties the tubes of areas
foul pleasure in bridges
the sight or thought of dive assorted to taxonomies
elemental oozing to figure indecent descent
crying on the train windows marks the blunt end of youth-
ful parades of flight

napes and skies have everything in common
exorcising monsters i exercise my imagination
well toned diverse fractals make the landscape
what all am i host to

days won't be needing those glasses
roots of trees deep in the walls (larynx)
so much opposite the sky endlessly dispensing
what were those parts of me called

barometer

don't believe you know
we passed on everyone familiar

pressure

without address public myth figure
the single child's constant
stranger's large countenance
lives the horror of unstoppable singularity
dark clouds invert this atmosphere
retreat to the birth canal
or simply inverse birth
january february march
march
march
my tiny 3rd arm waves to strangers
dreams aquariums
horizon's erased genitals

bray arcane while that goes on elsewhere
lark pumping wild in the cage
angled every night
stunned for mist or incident mandala
some falls when nodding
really is my schedule
to prioritize most
most
most
      squeezed:
subtle horizons re materializing
under winter rains and under my eyes
as you say the end of all your poems

can't come close to you in your way
otherwise i might momentarily
chew tenderly my tongue
old prophecies no help for stone
no meaningful testament
no clever fulfillment
my conception (cancellation) was perhaps that
distance

unreal flakes arrest the evening
watch crisp crystal dendrites prepare to melt
(*delicate* said the pursuer of the object)
in the pink orange reflected light
a revealing image of time   its annulment
supposed to search and find a definition for this

all i can do is think in sensation
desire   affirmation of flesh coin dream and vittle
the least useful continually pounding the inner ear
the most useful only impossible negotiations
everything is melting without end
(and elsewhere freezing)

                    arctic front
                    pacing
                    cracked ligaments
                    frozen relative
          we talk of tropics
                    like palaces
                                        every
                         movement a
                         meter at night
                    shims of neck
                    crystallized arteries

augh!

bounce your kiss off that sheering satellite
          my digits are
                    stuck
          in the permafrost
warm my lips with microwave
make my ears hot

                         exotic habit at

i'll draw a map of historic wind currents
      exact coordinates
       witnessed pressing fronts and measuring
      my machine recognized specific dna patterns
     hippocampus like a steel trap
    microchip keen on information and dust count
    the facts what i saw where i was
   the full term bright
   radiating with snow-locked flora
   cracking maple miscalculate
the weight on the branch before it broke the varying angles
pushed by the wind temperature's rise and fall the
weakening structure
     my own rigid skeleton functioning independently
     can't recall how it felt knowing the data

repine

stare at her belly

or nothing can survive this world

lunge
parry

particles reflecting the senses   maybe dark matter also
reflects   doctor is this my calligraphic zen again   still
symbols uncrashing and my body no less comes to
mind at two forty a.m.   standing steamed   platform
bound   the blood organ piping vodka and elements
soaking or rending my body at two forty five while
reflection as glory & how is it i shrug off
heiligenschein but imagine i've this severe lack of
imagination the debilitation of my society   someone
said over radio fade *your perspective product* and i
said fuzzy back and delayed *maybe all slavery*   how is
it that you have any interpretation of zen   i think no i
crave that affirmation of the root argument for my
sprawling optimism

fog aria

what draws from cover
for flesh or in the meal of it
shove up in action
twirling its pen
each octagon quiver
the megaphone
exit to enter that sigh
shaking ground or none
impermanence of current beds
wrap in the lip of proposition
hello

drag my petrified leg under me tonight humor and
nudity the essential humanity   what i need and will
most likely as if i were any closer to collapse but now
little consumption a little compulsion few smiles
fewer shoulders and how many determined for proof
of love yet no occurrence to offer   too complex to
specify in which way i am not contrary what do we
know of each other   intimate beg   the towel saturated
blue bit the sole note of self   how it curves or
resonates between our fleshed edifices or in each
particular location   the romantic nomadic ideal

isn't it true my darling that with certain
understanding any word is superfluous when it's
obvious it's now just you and i under this studded
canopy

                              the sun's hush warming your hair
                    while illuminating parts of my white sheets

is enough to make me sob in no spoken language
         don't ever

waiting

cardinal dash line

across
purple grey
drifting range

is it the
focus of light

when it collides
over an atmosphere

yellow of disintegration
any other season

the particles swell just before
schedule

eliminate flight
lucidly

your stinking gratuitous truth
everything falls on me but the thing
constantly absent green
constant hollow cadence
just look at you
look at you to finally not look for you
just shut up already
look at all your dumb books
look at you look at you

flip think where to go in this occurrence to hold self
back to regain or tickle over a particular plea to
prompt time as if that has much at all to do with any
particular plea if i had my way i'd mix up all the
exhibits and rearrange the molds a picture over my
own maybe ten more like my specific request since
the beginning of this period

in one dream my adult rode awkward down a
childhood street on kid's bike angrily yelling back at
gossip mongers in their fenced yard
there are no monsters but those who are in self denial

about as easy to find as local compassion or four leaf clover
string it up or fly
poetry   groceries   shock
tidal flies   thorn of coma
            spring

but i'm still sort of convinced the world is what you
make of it and i'm diligent doc so much so i will
lovingly call out your bestial name

i will locate locate   you i am locating you
(transforming)

44

the dark eye kid all agape
             agape2
             agape1

   keep my mouths open for
precipitation
             any gifts

        the kid's found, *hallelujah*
    alive in the mine shaft, *hallelujah*
        always the hole and the sky

(don't want anyone to see)
(elevator of sheets & lines)
a screen comes over our entire sphere
light point option
dream   as another annulment
did not exist   or again the mute foot forward
standard size
shells of my paranoia
shrieks of war or otherwise emptied sheets
nonrepresentational text!
war is foreign graffiti (to me)
never without relation to the big bowl above me
pictures of heads and guns and i am as well an image on a
ghetto wall
and incomprehensible subtext
(may not exist)

fickle hand relieved the atmosphere is so big from my l
ocation. when i'm otherwise pinned and sewn or just
dismembered.

what's most is no time to process or define what
makes another precious. wind from the midwest like
a gigantic hand taps us over.

it's not that i disagree with his thesis but that he must
sleep. beyond that i don't know what my child needs
any more.

gusts preceding tormenta might be responsible.
like in the dry bed of rio turia i looked up and
scattered.

conventional therapy might work for dysfunction but
not madness. there's a certain commitment humans
will make to complete their demise (or otherwise).

men have often considered genius excessive
organization or contrivance. i suspect neurosis
doesn't take as much intellect as time.

sense of integrity to work out this knot of knots.
innocent persistence of an ideal crazy high tide
laughter.

who is to blame for how white the sky is today.
everyone but the pair of mourning doves nesting
outside my bedroom window.

this entire time i'm trying to figure out molecular
reformation. i **am at times desperate and must have
it** immediately. *you don't look very   cohesive.*
to my filthy vagrant alter ego in my last dream.

            whirligig this mild day rose
        impossibly high above the valley
              against the most saturated

time dilation
circling dead leaves
shape of the wind
too sublime

wands:

microscope

telescope

periscope

kaleidoscope

beast generous

infinite
/   \
secrets   gifts

FROM SEA

a polyp is specialized for a sessile existence

don't remember which dreams are yours or mine
nonsense written on my nails at sea and held up
miniature projections of leaves on dreams or just memory
i don't remember writing letters to friends
and can't hear their shore stories but i'm trying to wave and
kind of smiling
line's elusive in rapid cycle
when i can't say *then and then*
but or and i and oar and slash
i was on a point once   something about the forecast
and everything was *experienced* FirstPerson

if not remembering not caring to distinguish or define
not enough to speak it but
cold rain and oranges
sometimes there's pyroclastic evidence of
yeah   submerged red fire

five minutes of said
you don't need so many words
every other can turn your life upside down
i follow my i/them stiffness
objectify every thing
blow me up
enemy words
unhinge my jaw
detached salvation
i've signed off from everything
don't need pills
images sufficiently translate time
rhythmic pattern i last
young and talk now only of myself
the thick cuff of the neck
we hallucinations
you are big and suffering
cry out for any true end or beginning
burnt hair
synaptic lightning

words will tell themselves
the little monsters
forgotten in two nights
hand printed exaggerations
which serendipitous light might believe me
i don't because the room echoes
clocks growl louder than i listen
far off more craggy banks
there's no proper way to speak
no reason to
it doesn't always play well to lighten up

      chattel
      fat old wife

self constrict red film thunder
choke sinister practice with figures
display palms
root out or under
do childish
image trickery primitive seizure timepiece
hours fruition symmetric isolation
faded content
survive this stake
grain fed   not completely
more particles longer wavelengths

avoid those isolation points
black like blue planet gaze
shuddering between atmospheres
capacity to ignite

unlike the cosmos this doomed area doesn't after all expand

geometric spectrum half the hole
above the reef
leaves torn scattered things
escaped parakeets flock
trapped in the weather
giant skyscapes remind of out
i'm halfway there tasting salt
could linger for half a year in decay
rain   waves drive sand briefly up
an insect scouting my departing topography
don't the raptors consider lifting me

thankfully
illumination of that cloud
most challenging to render

true horizon littered with light of ships
clutter of the metal groans
not enough rubber or vigilantes to protect us
creatures
the sky on the other hand
is astoundingly indifferent
we relish this amnesia gift
                                        stop

let loose the lions of the sea
set the sharks ashore
or no blood is unbearable
let's just not be born so often
                                        stop

inset with silence in mind
or no don't invent purge
what justification but enlightenment
                                        stop
we can forget useless amendments

never know why
to push
love is aggressive wind in your face
and none is just as much
my bones shatter out here asking for every thing
supply controller how many points to investigate
one life how badly
names in the poles slush joints
mechanical childhood of profound experiential ability
what coordinates sextant
missing darting figures of dust out here
and play of shadow
can't name any object any more

what is that

what is this

                    how do i say this

fixate
little bit
click on our metal hull
the rain's uncome
signals fire from time's machine
overcast change and accumulation of then
their small glories
turn to trust
magician's endless handkerchief trail
never near salt dear
the thing's splayed as bones
days roam and all that entails

s hrimp
e xcrement
a lexandria

blind and blind or drowning
harbor light smothered late
whips and tails
scythes for punks

my old man makes jokes in my shiny metal
jaw punctures throat
those parts of me are clearly
one-way caverns

it's clear i tend toward
that certain look skyward
nothing materializes either place
my stories locked up with me

when i go homogenous   dankly so
how much symbiosis and not *human*
all i suspect
why feed creatures

some hope like my old man
golden rule tide return
but one must live longer than this
for now   the world *as is*

not in this black ink floating lights spokes of moving
parts on the black hemisphere floating frothing black
can't back pointed yellow having lights always
distant moving in floating nest ink and some yet a
few distant skating slow as in slowly by and not
through or to reply recline in muting ink water of
black outside blackened windows naked light points
in your brighter clearings slowly passing ink black
absolute black another ground shadow prefix taking
out of the eyeball this diffraction while my inside
mudded deeply dark and speakers arrange banking or
surrounding the light are mute yellow as yellow as
my saltwater wounds or gills or vents inking

cinch
escapade
bramble
timeless hour
crawling over the dawn's edge
nothing critical about oranges
there's no edge
that's said

wry corner
most witness the movement to believe
all the virtual intimacies

can't trust someone to a trophic process
(don't you do well)
tail chaser of that thought and follow certain rules
(not know this love prohibition)
give me taurine and tequila
(to call mercury valid & dance around fires)
i feel ousted thinking to myself
(stop as in stop speaking command)
this belongs in another season another part of the
world
(mid sentence starts and fits ethic dictation)
the colors squeeze all sides
(now is rude now is polite but mostly what is)
breath caught in severed billows
(invisible cold front excess wind)
emphysemic trap   blasted
(couldn't get enough make it up)
vatted
(ask nicely)
sea is something to destroy yourself for
(can't take you seriously)
there's protocol
(need more blank pages)

take off bands red rags
careful what to fear
what if i stopped juggling
it's the only way to carry so many objects
count
down
every
reason

put to death the bed of learning
        put to bed the death of learning

optimal range
obliterate the old world
Fatima,
my wound
light responds
foreign guerrilla
bloody in the freeze
you will fall so too
from swamp to swamp
trail fortunes or grackles
anything that slides down the gullet
is worth the price
bodies in motion
i can't just now
rigor mortis shuffle
you must find the fluid connections

running nitrogen
tanks laid along trade routes
humans aggrieved for the aggrieving
become turned in two or another's
carved luxury these some with waiting
sonar ticks or debris over six floors
more
faults gaping in impatient grunt
likely excuse! mammals
turned in two deep running
they're carved so anxiously
exchange gasses ready
interminable gestures if not mixed
symbols aright ambient channels
hard fixed below frame
ex unguent or pixilated
whichever over turned hand
bathe top of sky blocked emulation
bestial follows the circle of
which what will i take
cathedral heights coral steeples jagged to catch
flash of forms open the switch
the sender trust twisting on high wire
slime eels don't know enough to curse
circumstance unwieldy
domesticate those creatures immediately!
truncated invertebrates kneel mightily
so hand-bound
grinning the blank spot
which colors our dialog bends upward
from crush pressure
static! cry the shrimp
static! the ship
static! again
we don't like how this comes out!

please stand back
light points grace below
white yellow red
a zone between high way gaze
lit structures
current shimmer
difficult to connect with a stolid heart
light row
dormant account
vertigo stomach until the possible lullaby

degrees of horizon slither past

awhile since contact
                      stop
as soon as gesture to paper
never respond
must stretch these bones no reason to happen
can't tell i've this hammer on my heel
for days and i don't search anymore
nothing comes of its own
stop
some say because of spine or scales the reason
but i admire the drive of the nautilus

of eye   of the ear
of the maladjusted line
how were you made
first protean
couldn't live without knowing
as if constellations or vapors prove any thing
more than your sensual faculty

we keep time too rigidly
some matter requires sustained perception
some sentences should be blinked
I'm tempted to visit the future for my benefit

                          alter

deep in the blood cells call for ordinary
which words pop or tunnel direct with association
i'd rather it leap and surprise of course

topics range from lore to tendril penetration
                                and oven cleaners
or extermination of general varmints
                                that seem too smart

        presorb me with the very real situation
                of running in place

it   the sky   *was steaming* again
but in an orange stew between the lower clouds
                of purple or a touch of terrible pink
                                and mostly gunmetal

the color of things i wish to shoot
        several times several times

it will fail
luggage fallen from insight and phrase

desert line drums the landscape
illustration of now

deep clouds
rate of change

silhouettes of anything organic
light hidden behind their movement paralyzes

blasphemous master placate me now
ripping against my face with vague syntax
what strikes real in-to you

there are stances to learn
against superstition's warrior
choose weapons wisely or be insignificant

struggle for dialog with yearning shadows
let me capture images to demonstrate my argument
proof of my red attempts
some movements studied

this is where she again desires a boating or
bathing interruptions of failure

don't track your children's moral stories of it
make that real skill
take a sledge hammer to your thin mast
and set your rudder afire
slash your *this is what the body can do*
split the brazen hull in two
don't cough above me or giggle in the sea
sear your clichés
let silence finally steal the breath of words
from your lips
you've everywhere to go
i've none   refuse to listen to me

cyclones common
eating eggs
dissent
forget about it
re-submerge

no markers
turning point
various current explanations
reasonable
for this behavior

can't conjure up appeal
or sustain that level
age tends to diminish
concern for definition among countless other concerns
to manage balloon process
or sea floor crawl
don't need to know beyond this forever action
my boring adjectives
no objects or objectives
but abduction disjunction adjunction abjection

over the falls but mostly
under them still harbor
vitriol for not if there seems a-tension

charismatic spectrum
rains every accomplishment coats now
preparation
optimize better sky
sepia seeping
intimate phrases nostalgic
or just as it yesterday
won't take less than reciprocity of desire
too for chasing tangents

(unstoppable rain how the point descend   subjugate
swagger like of the flirtatious mean the moon isn't
half there in my crease where we spent time to
convince me that even demise isn't so annulment of
idea we need an aesthetic of this where the work is
fully positioned in an instant infant seed soaking in
brine lit from symbiotic gesture our metamorphosis is
only change not youth or uncontact)

everyone's uncovered
hold this   a child reaches
do you think you would do better?
don't admit the reason for the falling sky
crystalline gears stick in the hair
time's come undone again
every time i'm in the bath

muted din of air's continual watery escape
i forget all of your names!
items have unmoored
brine stomach and torn algae
there is no sky where the sky was
it's only a color
a color remains
it's turned into a color
the definition for sky is this color
i'd kill for sight of a tree

push & pull
productivity might be how much we refrain
directed silence
armature   sacrifice

whole coordinate piece
can't remember the facts
what i saw   where i was
draw a map of it

as if a solid canopy
i'd dull slit it if i could
i'd detail on deck for days
all the proof of hate
how to defile that pristine cup

you sick fuck

all the way ward cells contact one way
those are the parts
names of my made-up compadres
sympatico gentle kelp with
letters on their lips
arrive in my lap
teeth and all
next stop elements reinforce in time
for my pre bath shower post midnight
sub bladder forced wait
cold sponge pant
windless
late interval abstract drawl
invented consonant (play)
airwave stability cavern structure
inspired fleet sweet tin cradle banging
leaving cruelty of disinfectant
black mirror welcome
infection is everything
cold thighs drying in the sparkle sound of glass
disengage from verb rut
threading topography complex hydrologic
think i'm shy

unlikely i'd find a full term psychopath just where i want
him   mud crying with trowel in hand

minimum requirement moment addiction to the addiction
the compass can't tie me to you or fight polarity

hints the depth of my depravity (fistulous)
you repeat three words in my head

does religion give you dignity
does history get you immortal

stare final stutter out for yes
this way to cruel convention

final glory slab too complex   .
butcher lions

shroud masticate trade wind nether
severance daze

props switch and characters switch plays
can't say a word with a straight face

pit serves the heights
glory draw blue sight upward

omphalos hum
corona suspension

what we say to each other dear
should never be poetic
ceiling end?
no expansion without sensual & intimate
relation of drifters' gain

divination:

      falling out of atmosphere
      how much care we are capable of
      structural collapse
      integrity defeated
      crumpled fins
      the lame arm in arm
      glubbing soporific
                there there

enough blown
erethism
hyperesthesia or none
tidal piling
afferent
efferent
pendulum needle red slice or white of eye or tooth
6 feet (fathom)
halo (ice crystal)
mean sea level
careen
straighten up
begin again

think through it
you're too much
don't speak
volition swamp of stench
think of all the tides (rides)
and the hulls in bogs
there's the Sargasso Sea
with its skeletons
adrift on a plane
floating between direction
I'm exhausted come clean
to my image
I predict you with papers
give you uses

current swinging the creature beneath the polarity
he hoped to find about his longing
                                                    but couldn't phrase a question
blood to his brain next step is to blur the seconds
                                            o that's right
what kind of dead mother won't show herself
                                            in a puddle or a purple cloud

                                            the children sat very still
                                            in their seats when the
                                            stellar wind blew way
                                            back

how do you
make an ideal one
align your current

000   all
water air penumbra
buoyancy
wasteful regret
stroke's reach and pull
and the wind's shift
braided string encircles
too beautiful to endure
capacity to love
this single element traverses
the still form emergent prostrate
to love   and to love oxygen
and whoever found it
and whoever named it
always the water and the air

i will bomb it tomorrow and there will be just now
                    this disappearance
so the words they are sunk charts are needed now
                    more than ever

or no.
cataclysm

mars will effectively
            as back-up

                    my toxic blueprint under his heel

open indigo close
some caught timeless in the undertow
foreign letters
meaningless warnings
mad intent
mind pool to the comfort
passe sun god
poor sponge indefinitely cut off
dead thing rubbed at the dead end body
sad clam profundo

wretched image
no reply again
who supports living inside a bubble

                                              arbitrary
                                            placement

                              victim
        bust
                ringing
pathology

biology's hopefulness
tissue's patience
                    locked on   intent
the wolf's forever winter stalk
                    tender
no image in atmosphere
only color to absorb

how to become a skilled cephalopod

charger
resolve
brn envelope
docs on blk file
blk emulsives
3 pt perception
miscellaneous
permits
nerve
capacity
swt spots
jetspeed
paper tablet and ink
practice with bowling pins or
balls or chnsaws or flaming stcks axes no guns!
guns and skeet!
flsafe

implode

      explode

implore

      explore

FROM SKY

some are prone to give themselves up prematurely
wish to be discovered dismissed disappeared

solace of photon diffusion
oasis of white noise

maybe the burden of decision discovery thought
too great for the invisible

everything dries out here
    tables
    tablets
    tableaus
    pictures
    one is another
    eyes
        voicebox

close your eyes

exhale

i'm plowed through
this big wall between warm & cold fronts

extremities
lay waste

it's not me
they don't believe me
not a word
anyway i prefer friends with integrity

what's in the air
don't stop here
in the buffer plane

    lost in the fog of sound
    keep moving through

she took out her thumb

    what is 'electric'

self image
    ideogram
    stripped down ego

burden of discovery's too heavy for the invisible

    azure claim
    so-called truth

some are prone to give themselves up prematurely

    good faith
    stamina
    sustenance

    here take anything
    take everything

name it
major movement in my little life

    what gives

there's no timer up here
it's beside the point
this is above the filters
you can hear proof
wind is what's left after all
though i swear i hear words

> *Chechnya…*
> *Slovenia…*
> *Afghanistan…*
> *Sudan…*

though can't recall what they mean

burrs attaching to my heels
know i'm leaving

> *don't forget me don't forget us*
> *when you go into the big world*
> *when you put on your fancy shoes*
> *and attend soirees   art openings &*
> *business luncheons*

i pick them off my arches & toes
preferring they do this the rest of my life
than that i go out
into the big world
one more day

if we had more choices
timers would be pliable venn diagrams
and i'd squeeze out the sap
from my sponge heart
a little more often

c i v i l i z a t i o n   o n   h o r i z o n

weather review:

september	knocked the wind out
october	power blackout
november	clarified news of impending winter
december	blow to the back of the head

you asked for it

forecast

get up punk

traipsing around above it all
brushing lackadaisical
circumnavigation notes
process to process
forget my perhaps glaring lessons-in-waiting

oh well

another arc fault full stop

once pet the cheap brochures & re-read the adverts
yearned every summer riding near
never stopped at the mystery spot
though it was clear on the map
all roads tangled around the big purple question
mark   my kid heart

i think i know what that soil feels
sd the pouting cloud

your phantom voices rich in my neck
some of yr characters too visit splitsecond

some distant clouds resemble old lovers reclined
feeling loving arms of friends virtual

    ready when you are

extract fruit juice from thin air
the way ink runs thin on the skin
on the side of the hand
rain like me passing through old home during layover

making list of eliminations & leaving
in foreign receptacle
making list of new fittings
keeping it snug to my ass
        i'm a one man band

        i see yr beautiful face often
        with my hands too

all the tongue alone could sense
brain not registering
keep scrubbing and rinsing
it's just time for this

    salt
    sweet
    bitter
    sour

dear dad,

just escaped death valley
maybe the last time

spires of salt
a flash flood

my canary swept away
  it all came out in the wash

i'm a supersensor
no victim of the elements this time

there were sailing boulders
believe it

wing muscle mnemonic

forget what it's like to pace a cage
    when the bird's lying eye goes blind

when the good stories materialize
weather's inconsequential   .

she flies over all the oceans finally

gripping phenomenon   broken open egg of brain or
heart   that's where or why   number   play old times
relentless   not budging   move over   all i dreamt about
was taxes   make way the convolution of puzzle
solving and loved ones   all points on the hidden map
isolated grudges   mingle other vowels   better left
alone   much better when brow's covered this eking
out makes me uglier & my world too   running the
risk of rushing completely   writing should allow
living without so much entanglement but it's the
opposite in mind   humour under covers   when the
heart's storming or battering fuselage i'm crawling
where oh where's my hole in the rock

release the murder of misspellings
it's getting hotter for longer

fearing all sorts of shortages
i sleep with one hand on my pen

      wrest
          watch

perspective's inaccurate
branching habit the all pervading fractal

usual sets of maps and topographies
so-called "west" and so-called "south"

more dusty roads and struggling rivers below
these quiet storms move in & out too quickly

my head pops out micro-dendrites like a machine
& chromatophores are aching again   a lot

vagabond vegetation
there go four death wishes
one more
& one yet behind me   impatiently revving

it'll pass
sd john in another life when hugging me goodbye

i'm the sun devil over tucson mountains
the palo verde and cholla companions
          this sublime isolation

thanksgiving postcard featured
drawing of a naked man at a table looking up
a loaf with a sun symbol
clouds
one black others with thick black outlines
a goddess [eos] riding pegasus [lightning] in the distance
and two cherubim also with thick black outlines

he wrote the family

> *I don't need much*
> *this here sky*
> *a loaf of bread*
> *and these clouds*

something in russian

> *and for Carl to be well*

*as a diviner he wasn't appreciated in his own country

pine
pinus ponderosa
Pinus brachyptera Engelm
strunt
barren
cambium
turpentine
pitys
song
quickly growing taproot
impressive lateral system

basal fire scars common in old growth

medicinal uses:
antiseptic; diuretic; febrifuge; ophthalmic; pectoral; poultice;
rubefacient; salve; skin; vermifuge;
vulnerary

prescription eliminating particular
inclinations leant insight
turned out to be a live wire

very serious absurdity lay in & beneath this artifice
what are we without it but to perpetuate human reign

shed layers of past psych
pare down the fancies *tone it down*

victim role
keep to theater of memory

palette of sadness
only for philanthropy or profit

sacrificial acts
mind the bottom line & percentages

bring on true desire so to endure
natural enhancement to power change

tho isn't lightning romantic
& think of the nitrogen

leaving the substories
woes of or in flight
rib cage cranked open
your heart finally exposed to open air
quivering take-off

    are we finished yet

timbre of your voice hasn't changed
for my entire life
now with attendants over phone
brings me to tears
throat its own creature
tightens
measures everything
by number of certainties

        open the gates
        let it rumble up

sorry been elsewhere

been drawing granite footing & reconstructing
with blue light

                                        picnic   soon

all of my meanings are your meanings and mornings
dawn has a sharp flavor especially above the clouds
sun is a wall of love with quick jabbing approach

surfing is to skip between the possible meanings
stretch a little between words you'll get my meaning
negate histories (other) for a moment at least

after learning to categorize
there's necessity of dissonance arrangement
no worries hang loose

what evolutionary purpose of being enamoured
with man's wit
your puns belie

redeemers like nina-ma & kali-ma
perfectly illustrate the tough girl wish
twisted up like a true true punk to shake your shit

not so much the water reflects
the sand on the shore reveals
all that was once invisible

patterns emerge only in context
or start a new one
maybe like

invitation for invitation
i have my story
i think i'll have a story

edge of grand
sounds like we've got folded phrases between us
how it comes out
jet stream crossing
even breathing & another new moon
longest red marks the clumsy beginning
over something
under

keep sleeping & waking to the same sunset

indentations (sleep)
(rivers) (beds) (gullies)
(wind) (rains)
foreigner with headphones
cistern dreams   high plains
(cells)

approaching mountains front line stratus
we're trying to outrun the persistent planet
small warm beacons
beckon below
        in from the cold

drone drowns out my or whomever's narration
always grateful for the rare oblivion

oh, gee   *i'm here*

make light of strife

lightning cracks across the horizon
early morning to late

    seriously now

how does this work

     boots on or *off*

this is all a deal with the devil

must sit with all the contradictions
              woeful poet, reconcile brain & heart

still through living
behind the wing
refuel (kill)

strewn about the forest below
fine remains
another one of those things

              as humanly possible

a hand at the window
keep an eye out for the dark grift

register discolor striated rolls
mounds the clouds skirt
kids at mothers' knees
thirty thousand cruising lines
countless burdens all in all
how is it now   best in years
super eighty capacity

here barely by robotic knuckles
laborious flight crying on airplane panes
no options but to follow itinerary & delays
exercising the f l o w muscle

ascent   descent
pressure on heart squeezes out eyes
clamping   sinus to suppress guts coming out eyes
lakes are welcome sight for sore eyes spewing green
not gonna stay here anymore
huffing through the sky
          no matter what

safety instructions pass down the aisle
i refuse to memorize mythologies
build my own by default like that stupid face mask
"to start the flow of oxygen" &
"breathe normally"
my tenuous relation
sensitive SENSITIVE

accelerated change clears
nothing but the wingspan &
states fractured with topographical veins
healing in grief waves
tolerate distraction
less than this
more than a decade shooting over
last swarm
cells slough a different person
but for the echo

116

mysterious geometries sway ahead
quickening horizon
leave the devices airborne

exactly this altitude
fields   farm houses
like in so many dreams

blinding dull light
music might make it bearable
ignore surrounding mediocrity

engine drones medulla
push through it
push   push   push

you flagged a trail for divinity
       to mark the place for arduous drilling
       opportunity for light to move through

    rather one big smudge hovering around

              masíah
              ghrei
              grime
              cresme
              creme
              gris
              grim
              grey

       all names of one child ghost

isolating wind around the formative years
third eye slimed and loaded
marinated girl gone glossolalium
eyelids mysterious exit strategies
flagged place of (en)light entry (departure)
hands and voices alone always shone through
difficult portals
kid dragged around by leaded head
propelled by explosions

is this what you meant when you defined the babe
to invoke grace of your meaning

     in my world
         in my world
         my third eye projects all strangers

unquiet mind   undertow
timbre of surf

you painted after me
contrail
                what else to do

sitting looking at the sea
self respect may require sacrifices
to or of my credit

this sail jerks her high
slams her into the surf
a deepening thunder
                where did my head get to

what should have fallen
all through the last year
came down today
took everything loose out to sea

          the vegetable garden
          one hundred year-old trees
          litter
          teeth & other collectibles
          shards of too-bright memories
          slippers
          family photos
          snarls
          love notes
          grocery lists
          short pencils
          truncations

random number   i give

iq test for the tester
you can't generate a number
more complex than yourself

a thing's expression takes
vastly more information
than its information

there's no sign from another
you see only what you see

though superstition is a false compression
my deified image is intensely dense
with structure in an atmospheric blur

      phase space
      tidal force
      mega jets
      vortex holding

hold this trinity of inner peace in yr mouth for eons

            complexity
            chaos
        quantum uncertainty

no consolation dear me
mind possible frontal lobe malfunctions
repeating internal refrains have simply been distractions to
infernal externals

keep yr damn speakers in yr house
or i'll throw them at you

even visual noise shortens the breath
i hold it or blow it
here's not the place for me here's not the place

get yr freaking cards outta my books
and stay out

attempt to turn it off at the receptor
tho i note myself
curiously calmly reject
entire products with
patriarchies, mythologies, superstitions, neuroses,
canons, obdurate binary reasoning, demands,
proscription, convention, proselytization

& to mention the endless social performers
who negate the other of their obliging audience
not just tiresome to the burgeoning moth
proboscis politely wound   becoming very wobbly

i've never sat through a pharmaceutical convention
or kkk rally
but you get the sheer torture of listening

notes to read while in flight:

dear

fill out

for you

relax

new mountains

oh this is a new landscape to me

loved

right on time

buffer something internal

till internal

desert edge

so fond of you

irrigation lines

"hifting images

taciturn days

saguaro means sky

ecstatic madness
of sea forest mountain field

contagion of the enraptured
to perish in delight of
full moon & heilegenshein
calm sea & soil

overboard
overhead
laughter in drowning
in rolling

eyes overcome
sand underfoot

all options of its fusion

      crested
      wet
      ribbed
      raised
      warted
      powdered
      sponged
      rippled
      taut

            submit submit submit

blind scavenger hunt where
"up" here as transformation & nonlinear direction
orchestrate it like a demigod & forget about it
will's behind the knees not eyes

gnash in place and out of place
        give me my damn shroud back
        i gotta hunker down
        figure how to get outta this
suck tongue
        don't you ever shut your mouth
there are traveler's manners
        keep your delusions to yourself

desire's not paradoxical when understood
conventional desire
pretty fancies of sadness
[continue in a state of profound emotion
fear of triggering same eddy
fear of not desiring that which is lacking
conundrum: self-deprivation & evolution vs familiar]
        come on now reason
known hells or gratification in movement
comfort's simple perspective
        i want the ladder

H

H

H

H

H

oh to find the sail in the human slug

        oh, my snail!

landing up
shaken hammock station
twisted comfort of rocking
bough don't break
opened that chapter with a reeling feeling
pressurized door lock
suspended again in nausea
until the re-approach

counting that
owls do figure portals to anything else
infinite numbers of blackbirds happily
wave their good faith
in a theoretical physics state of mind

bullied heart by
twenty-two thousand feet
thirty thousand feet

anticipating the consolation of terra firma silence

you know

you know you left the sound of jets in my ears

moments between heard testimony
when reason's elusive
fallen through floor boards
sniffing obligation

nothing to say anywhere to anyone
sometimes say never
mortal morsels
you & me
here we are again

my books tell you too much
my conch
my peach

misfit   turn that leg out

it's not the void that infuriates you
it's me
i've done what i could
and here we are

intimacy of cemeteries
say what you like
familiarity breeds contempt
the usual way to be

please kindly disengage your gaze from me
nothing vital here
your unrelenting perception is a good mask

if you want to be so
crude crooners robins
& fish are the dogs of the sea

widows walk conversation with dusk

> *sanity's the ability to give coordinates*
> *& contextualize*

& so a dictum

is certainty so impressive
an arbitrary plane
is this right
like rightness   as in true as in flying
or altruism

experimentation is a process wherein we role play
allow our graphic to more freely form itself
even role-less

best naïve guru drops an affine space
knotted lattice in hand
self proclamation to adapt a vector
> *in all seriousness*

float down the river
eddy under a tree
write backwards
> *leef i woh si siht*

> *leef i woh si siht*

why not become right here right now
it's the stuffing the pulp
> *what you remember is your self*
one day could be a millennium
perfect sweet oblivion   to fuck off

[captain's musical v.o.]

> *lay down your burdens*
> *down by the riverside…*
grand canyon all the way down even from the
sky truly

cracked to swallow our hull maybe if all goes
that way

[captain's v.o.]

> *no more war*

it would be fine
all these ritual imaginings in flight
the safest distance to make real progress
distance one can feel
truly

[captain's v.o.]

> *you got to feel to heal*

deep sighs and ocular luggage, sacrifices
to the sky
god today

[captain's musical v.o.]

> *space and time*

> *…space and time and all that jazz*

LIGHTNING AND THUNDER
ALARM ALARM
THUNDER CRACKS ITS GIANT WHIP
OVER AND OVER AND OVER AGAIN
PERSISTENT STROBE OF EXTREME
LIGHTNING PERVASIVE
OF EVERY SHATTERED ATOM
EXTREME FUCKING LIGHTNING
VEXED FISSION

you creeping creature
soft hair
back of eyelids
floriferous
under brush

keep rubbing your eyelids
no more pouting
sky's on fire

try not averting baby
try this

multilingual   jesus h christ   in the meta sense

i mean

peel back your psychic blinds to beauty have strength
to tolerate beauty fortitude to engage beauty faith to
create beauty courage to acknowledge beauty risk
repeated use of beauty   perceive & conceive beauty

that's right   *blow your own mind*

blue on your fingers from the cosmic inkvine

flying over electric storm
theatre of strikes
watching poison billow through our pristine pool too
from muted long distance

going back to the end that could have been
didn't know i'd fall all the way back
to the broken asphalt in that alley
& vomit myself inside out

didn't expect to find a parallel on this round-trip
the image dissolved in quickening colors

dubious that anything can stay together at these
altitudes and speeds

                    rivet and intake

humans forgoing morse code seems overly confident

lightning assist:

-.-. --- ..- .-.. -.. / ..- .... . / ... --- -- . / ...
..- .--. . . .-. -. . .- - ..- .-. .- .-.. / .- -.. .... .
                ... .- .

native deity spies from behind a cloud
gull flies into its mouth   seemingly blowing
but not

    you left out some things

    yeah

the origin below knows all about what's going on
up here
this time we're having an intimate conversation

    why do you think you haven't left us yet

we both know how it's supposed to echo like this
for the rest of the weekend

landing billows back again to rest
welcome new aspects home again

old comparisons fall away in this atmosphere
we're finally to the safer sky finally
ebbing

these places freely encourage further

you've done it   we'll see

s   e   l   f   branching   o   u   t

Hassen Saker creates & performs
transmedia poetry with texts, photog-
raphy, video and sound. In addition,
she's a sustainable entrepreneur and
filmmaker. Saker has lived throughout
the U.S. & currently resides in the
Philadelphia area.

PRAISE FOR *SKY JOURNAL*

Hassen Saker's Sky Journal proposes three ways of getting to the heart of matter. In three sustained sequences ("From Land," "From Sea," "From Sky"), Saker "think[s] in sensation," admitting that she (we, any 21st-century subject) "must sit with all the contradictions" that method entails. The book begins in "From Land" with a visual and perhaps historical "elevation," a vantage from which to take in the view. But unlike the Romantic, who both surveys and defines the sublime from his own icy pinnacle, Saker carefully dismantles sublimity's power over language. Her "tormenta," the thunder and lightning that punctuate her researches and revelations, are both psychic and climatic, and yet they effect a gentle "glubbing soporific" humor, too. "Complexity/chaos/quantum uncertainty" devolve upon the " s e l f branching o u t " of the final section, certainly more invitation than conclusion. Invitation to "blow your own mind" (as she would have it)—or let Hassen Saker do it for you.

–Jean Day

Hassen Saker's *Sky Journal* is a book of destinies and losses, of ghosts and possibilities, of divination and continuity. The continuities Saker renders are complex, full of "difficult portals," "shards of too-bright memories," the "intimacy of cemeteries." These are "all points on a hidden map." While "everything is melting without end/(and elsewhere freezing" "words will tell themselves/the little monsters." Our guide wonders "now how to dredge the distressed heavens/of my words" and warns "stay away from the study of thought, son." This book is a repository and an invocation, made of meteorology and language and event, of creatures and of time; it is a place where news of foreign wars fit like "burrs" to our deaf feet, even as it is as well a seamless, motive place, like emotion and like weather. This is the struggle she proposes and narrates, bears witness to: the struggle to integrate so much information, with honor and with heart, because "we keep time too rigidly/some matter requires sustained perception."

–Elizabeth Treadwell

Sky Journal is an intricate and enigmatic work that juxtaposes, sometimes paralogically, degrees of solidity, qualities of light and color, and spectra of emotion. In it, there are "hundreds of miles of solid sky," "phosphorous things" and "succulent thought," "ethereal invertebrates," and "a rock I've loved" not too far from an "anemone." In it, "crystal dendrites prepare to melt." It calls stars both "breathing holes" and "branding irons." It calls into being "particles reflecting the senses maybe dark matter also…" … I daresay it's a work of physics…Listeners, please welcome the intensely focused fluid energy and three dimensional perspicacious magnifying glass that is hassen.

—*Nada Gordon*

DUSIE